© Copyright 2025 - All rights reserved.

The content contained within this book may not be reproduced, duplicated, or transmitted without direct written permission from the author or the publisher.

Under no circumstances will any blame or legal responsibility be held against the publisher, or author, for any damages, reparation, or monetary loss due to the information contained within this book, either directly or indirectly.

Legal Notice:

This book is copyright protected. It is only for personal use. You cannot amend, distribute, sell, use, quote, or paraphrase any part, or the content within this book, without the consent of the author or publisher.

Disclaimer Notice:

Please note the information contained within this document is for educational and entertainment purposes only. All effort has been executed to present accurate, up-to-date, reliable, and complete information. No warranties of any kind are declared or implied. Readers acknowledge that the author is not engaging in the rendering of legal, financial, medical, or professional advice. The content within this book has been derived from various sources. Please consult a licensed professional before attempting any techniques outlined in this book.

By reading this document, the reader agrees that under no circumstances is the author responsible for any losses, direct or indirect, that are incurred as a result of the use of the information contained within this document, including, but not limited to, errors, omissions, or inaccuracies.

Table of Contents

Introduction	1
Chapter 1: Early Egypt and the Old Kingdom	2
Chapter 2: The Middle and New Kingdoms	9
Chapter 3: The Third Intermediate Period and Later Period (1070 BCE-332 BCE)	18
Chapter 4: Daily Life in Ancient Egypt	25
Chapter 5: Land of the Pharaohs	31
Chapter 6: Egyptology: Mummies and Pyramids	41
Chapter 7: Language and Hieroglyphics	53
Chapter 8: Mythology: Gods and Goddesses	59
Chapter 9: Forty Fun Facts About Ancient Egypt	67
Conclusion	75
If you want to learn more about tons of other exciting historical periods, check out our other books!	76
Books to Check Out	77
References	78
Image Sources	79

INTRODUCTION

The ancient Egyptians created one of the first great civilizations in the world. But for thousands of years, much of their history and culture was buried beneath the desert sands. Thanks to archaeologists and historians, we now know much more about these fascinating people!

Still, ancient Egypt remains a land of mystery. Scientists and explorers continue to search for answers to questions. How did they make mummies? Why and how did they build the pyramids? Who were the powerful rulers of Egypt?

Giant statues, towering pyramids, and ancient temples give us clues about the gods, goddesses, and pharaohs the Egyptians worshiped. Modern research into their world began over a hundred years ago, but there is still so much to discover!

Have you ever wondered why the Egyptians made mummies? Or if the legendary "mummy's curse" is real? Why do some paintings of pharaohs show them with animal heads?

In this book, you'll travel back in time to explore the incredible world of ancient Egypt. You'll learn about the great rulers of the Early, Middle, and New Kingdoms. You'll discover their amazing inventions, artwork, and monuments.

What was life like for Egyptian children? Did they go to school? What games did they play? What kinds of food did families eat? You'll find the answers to these questions and more!

This book is packed with fun facts, pictures, and activities to help you experience the wonders of ancient Egypt. Are you ready to step into the past? Then let's go!

Chapter 1: Early Egypt and the Old Kingdom

The people of ancient Egypt built their homes and cities along the Nile River in northeastern Africa. The land near the river was **fertile** (*fur-tile*), meaning it was great for growing crops. Because of this, the Egyptians were able to farm and live there for thousands of years!

The ancient Egyptians planted crops for food, created their own spoken and written language, and made **laws** (rules) to govern their society. They worshiped many gods and goddesses in their temples and built pyramids. Some of these pyramids still stand today!

Who Ruled Ancient Egypt?

Egypt was usually ruled by powerful kings. At times, no single ruler was in charge. We call those periods the **Intermediate Periods**. The First Intermediate Period lasted about 100 years after the Old Kingdom. The Second Intermediate Period lasted about 150 years after the Middle Kingdom. During these times, Egypt had no strong central ruler. Different leaders controlled different areas.

During the Old, Middle, and New Kingdoms, Egypt was ruled by kings or pharaohs (*fair-ohs*). The rulers of Egypt came from **dynasties** (*dine-as-tees*), which were families that held power for many years. Some dynasties lasted for hundreds of years!

> **Fun Fact**
> Egyptians only started calling their kings pharaohs during the New Kingdom.

Other Civilizations

Egypt was not the only great civilization at the time. In **Mesopotamia** (*mess-oh-poh-tame-ee-ah*)—a region in the Middle East—other cultures thrived. Some of these civilizations might have **influenced** (changed or inspired) the Egyptians.

Some important groups from Mesopotamia included:

- **Sumerians** (*soo-meh-ree-uhnz*): They were the first people to create a written language, doing so around 3000 BCE.
- **Akkadians** (*uh-kay-dee-uhnz*): They might have been the first people to develop the idea of kings.
- **Elamites** *(ee-luh-mites):* They lived in what is today Iran. They were traders, artists, and jewelry makers.

Ancient Sumerian writing.[1]

The Three Kingdoms of Egypt

Thanks to **archaeology** (*aar-kee-aa-luh-jee*)—the study of ancient times—historians have learned a lot about how ancient Egyptians lived.

Historians have divided ancient Egypt into three main time periods:

- The Old Kingdom (c. 2686–c. 2181 BCE)
- The Middle Kingdom (c. 2055–c. 1650 BCE)
- The New Kingdom (c. 1550–c. 1070 BCE)

The Old Kingdom (c. 2700–c. 2200 BCE)

At first, Egypt was divided into two parts. There was **Upper Egypt** (southern Egypt) and **Lower Egypt** (northern Egypt). Towns and villages were built along the Nile River, which stretches over four thousand miles!

FUN FACT

" About 95 percent of Egypt is desert, but nearly all Egyptians (even today) live within two miles of the Nile River. "

A king named Narmer is believed to have **united** (brought together) Upper and Lower Egypt into one kingdom. He made **Memphis** (a city in northern Egypt) the capital. The Nile River helped Egyptians travel, trade, and connect with other places like the Mediterranean Sea and the Red Sea. They traded food, gold, tin, and stone for building.

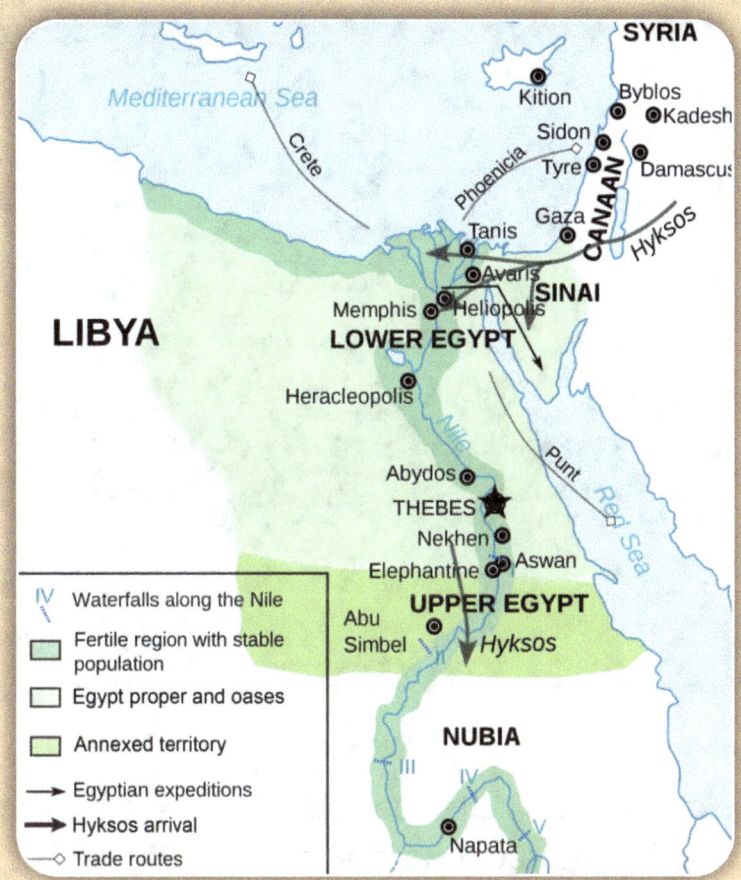

Map of Upper and Lower Egypt.[2]

Egyptian Writing and Monuments

The Egyptians invented **hieroglyphs** (*high-row-gliffs*), a writing system made up of pictures. Many stories from the Old Kingdom were carved into stone. Hieroglyphs help us learn about ancient Egyptian history.

One of the most famous kings of the Old Kingdom was Djoser (*joe-zer*). Around 2630 BCE, he ordered the building of the Step Pyramid, the first pyramid ever built! This pyramid was designed by his vizier (*vuh-zeer*), Imhotep. The Step Pyramid was the tallest building of its time.

The Step Pyramid.[3]

Egyptian kings didn't rule alone. They had a **vizier**, a trusted advisor who helped them run the country. Viziers helped the king make decisions, enforce laws, and manage the government.

> **Fun Fact**
>
> " Imhotep was so important that later Egyptians even worshiped him as a god of wisdom and medicine! "

Another famous king, Khafre (*ka-fruh*), ruled from 2570 to 2544 BCE. He built the second-largest pyramid at Giza. It still stands today! Khafre is also believed to have built the Great Sphinx, a huge statue with the body of a lion and the head of a king. Many believe the face of the Great Sphinx was modeled after Khafre himself.

The Great Sphinx at Giza.[4]

The End of the Old Kingdom

As time went on, some kings became weaker. They struggled to keep Egypt united. Different local rulers took control of parts of Egypt. This led to a period of chaos and change called the First Intermediate Period.

After many years, a new ruler, Mentuhotep II (*men-too-ho-tep*), brought peace to Egypt. He started the Middle Kingdom, which we will learn about in the next chapter.

Chapter 1 Activity

Fill in the blanks with the correct answer.

1. The ancient Egyptians lived along the banks of the _____ River.

    (Amazon, Niger, Nile, Yellow, Yangtze)

2. There were _____ primary periods (kingdoms) of ancient Egypt.

    (2, 3, 5, 6)

3. The _____ are believed to have created the first written language.

    (Egyptians, Chinese, Mesopotamians, Sumerians)

4. The word _____ means the study of ancient times.

    (history, hieroglyphs, archaeology, exploration)

5. King _____ is believed to be the face of the Great Sphinx of Giza.

    (Imhotep, Djoser, Khafre, Narmer)

Chapter 2: The Middle and New Kingdoms

The Middle Kingdom was the second major era of ancient Egyptian history. During this time, the Egyptian people became more skilled builders and designers.

After the Old Kingdom ended, Egypt entered a period of fighting. The northern Egyptians battled the southern Egyptians. Eventually, a powerful king from Upper Egypt reunited the country.

> **Fun Fact**
> "The Nile River flows from south to north. This is why Lower Egypt was in the north, and Upper Egypt was in the south."

Mentuhotep II ended the fighting and united Egypt. He ruled for about fifty years. Mentuhotep moved Egypt's government center to Thebes, a city in Upper Egypt.

> **Fun Fact**
> "Thebes is famous for the Valley of the Kings, where many ancient pharaohs were buried."

Painted image of Mentuhotep II.[5]

At first, Mentuhotep's rule was peaceful. He strengthened the government by sending officials across the country to ensure that local leaders followed his laws. He also expanded Egypt's military and built great tombs and temples.

However, not all of Mentuhotep's rule was peaceful. He fought against **Bedouins** (*beh-deh-wins*), a group of **nomads** (people who move from place to place) who lived in desert areas around the Nile Delta. To protect Egypt from invaders, he built forts along Egypt's borders.

One of the last great rulers of the Middle Kingdom was Amenemhat III (*ah-men-em-hat*). He ruled alongside his father, Senusret III (*seh-noos-ret*), before becoming king on his own.

Amenemhat III helped Egypt become wealthier. He created a new irrigation system near modern-day Cairo, making more land suitable for farming. He also encouraged mining, especially for turquoise in the Sinai Mountains. Egyptians mined stone from quarries (*kwor-eez*) to build stronger cities, temples, and tombs.

Statue of Amenemhat III.⁶

Despite these successes, the Middle Kingdom did not last forever.

The End of the Middle Kingdom

When Amenemhat III died, he was followed by his son, Amenemhat IV. His reign was short. When he died, Sobekneferu (*soh-bek-nef-er-oo*), the first known female pharaoh of Egypt, took the throne. She ruled for a few years, but after her death, there was no strong leader to take her place.

This led to a time of weaker kings and struggles for power. Many pharaohs ruled for only a short time, and Egypt became divided. As the central government weakened, foreigners known as the Hyksos (*hick-sos*) moved into northern Egypt. They slowly gained control and later became the rulers of Lower Egypt. The Hyksos admired Egyptian culture and adopted many of its traditions.

> **FUN FACT**
> " Historians believe the Hyksos came from Canaan (modern-day Israel and Palestine), but no one knows for sure! "

This period of Egyptian history is called the **Second Intermediate Period**. It lasted for about one hundred years. Egypt was divided again. The Hyksos ruled the north, and the Egyptians in Thebes ruled the south. Another group, the Nubians, controlled land farther south.

During this time, Egypt did not produce as much great art, writing, or architecture as it had during the Middle Kingdom. Instead, there was constant fighting and distrust between the Egyptians and the Hyksos.

Eventually, Egypt regained control over its land. This marked the beginning of a powerful new era: the New Kingdom.

The New Kingdom (c. 1550-1070 BCE)

During the New Kingdom, Egypt became stronger and more powerful than ever before. Pharaohs expanded Egypt's lands, and trade grew, bringing in new goods from faraway places. Scribes and important officials kept records and wrote down laws, stories, and religious texts.

The first pharaoh of the New Kingdom was Ahmose I (*aa-mowz*). He made sure Egypt's borders were protected, preventing future invasions.

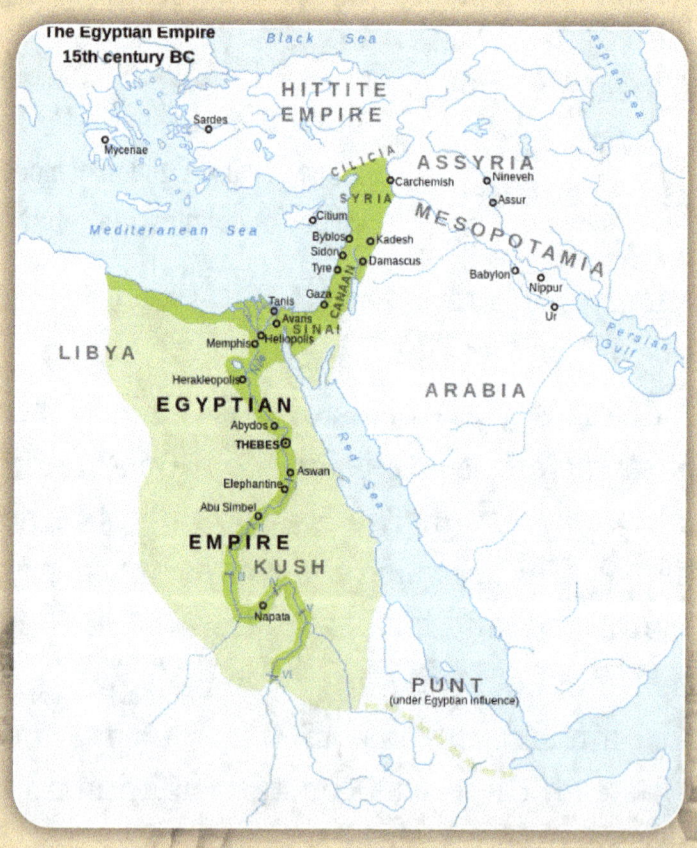

Map of the New Kingdom.[7]

As the New Kingdom grew, the pharaohs built a strong **monarchy** (a government system where one ruler had all the power). The military expanded, and the Egyptians developed better weapons, including chariots and bronze swords.

Famous Pharaohs of the New Kingdom

Amenhotep I

After Ahmose I, his son, Amenhotep I, became pharaoh. He expanded Egypt's borders and ordered the construction of many temples and monuments.

Hatshepsut (ruled c. 1479 to 1458 BCE)

One of the most famous pharaohs of the New Kingdom was a woman. Her name was Hatshepsut (*hat-shep-soot*). She ruled after her husband, Thutmose II, died.

Hatshepsut was a successful leader who focused on peace and trade instead of war. She built many temples and strengthened Egypt's economy. However, her stepson, Thutmose III, did not like that she had ruled instead of him. After she died, he tried to erase her memory by destroying statues and images of her.

> **Fun Fact**
> "Hatshepsut was one of seven female pharaohs in Egyptian history. The last was Cleopatra!"

Thutmose III (ruled c. 1479 to 1425 BCE)

Thutmose III was known as one of Egypt's greatest military leaders. Unlike Hatshepsut, he was warlike and led many military campaigns. He expanded Egypt's lands to the east and south, making Egypt larger than ever before.

Akhenaten (ruled c. 1353 to 1336 BCE)

Akhenaten (*ahk-nah-ten*) changed Egypt's religion. He made people worship only one god, **Aten**, the sun disk, instead of many gods. He built a new capital called Amarna and closed temples dedicated to the old gods.

Many Egyptians did not like these changes. After Akhenaten died, his ideas were erased, and the Egyptians returned to their old religion.

Ramesses II (ruled c. 1279 to 1213 BCE)

Ramesses II (*ram-uh-seez*) was one of Egypt's most powerful pharaohs. He ruled for sixty-six years! He fought many battles, including the Battle of Kadesh, which led to one of the first peace treaties in history. He built huge temples, like Abu Simbel (*aa-boo sim-bel*), and had over one hundred children. Because of his long and successful reign, he is often called Ramesses the Great.

Part of the massive temple of Ramesses II, Abu Simbel.[8]

We will learn about more famous pharaohs in Chapter 5!

The End of the New Kingdom

The New Kingdom flourished for almost five hundred years, but eventually, things began to fall apart.

The pharaohs lost power, and local leaders took control in different regions. Even though Egypt's military had been strong, the economy weakened. Over time, Egypt lost its power and wealth. This marked the end of the New Kingdom.

Although later rulers tried to bring back Egypt's former glory, the country was never as powerful as it had been during the New Kingdom.

Chapter 2 Activity

Each group of sentences contains two truths and one lie. Circle the lie.

1.

a. During the Middle Kingdom, Egypt was always at peace.

b. Mentuhotep II established his rule at Thebes.

c. Hatshepsut was a famous female pharaoh during the New Kingdom.

2.

a. The Hyksos people lived in Egypt for a long time before they took over parts of Egypt.

b. The Bedouins made many houses and towns throughout Egypt during the Middle Kingdom.

c. During the Middle Kingdom, the borders of Egypt were not strong.

3.

a. The New Kingdom was one of the strongest periods in the history of ancient Egypt.

b. During the New Kingdom, the king of the land was called a pharaoh.

c. Thutmose III is believed to be the pharaoh who caused the demise of the New Kingdom.

Chapter 2 Activity Answers

1. A is the lie.
2. B is the lie.
3. C is the lie.

Chapter 3: The Third Intermediate Period and Later Period (1070 BCE-332 BCE)

After the New Kingdom ended, Egypt became weak again. This era of Egyptian history lasted about four hundred years. What happened?

After the death of Pharaoh Ramesses XI in 1070 BCE, Egypt became less stable. As before, different regions along the Nile River tried to rule themselves. It did not work well. Local leaders fought for power, and Egypt became divided.

During these years, many customs changed. The way people were ruled was different. Leaders of big cities like Thebes and Hermopolis constantly competed for control.

Because Egyptians were too busy fighting each other, they could not stop foreign rulers from taking over.

INTERESTING FACT

Droughts and famine also led to the decline of the New Kingdom.

One of the kingdoms that took over Egypt was Kush. The people of Kush lived south of Egypt in what is today Sudan. The Kushites (also known as Nubians) ruled Egypt as the Twenty-fifth Dynasty from around 747 to 656 BCE.

The Assyrians (*uh-seer-ee-uhns*) came next. They ruled from around 671 to 663 BCE. The Assyrians came from Mesopotamia. Their army was stronger than Egypt's, and they invaded several cities, including Memphis.

The Assyrian army attacking Memphis.[9]

These years were filled with wars and invasions. Egypt was no longer united, and its power had faded. Because of this, the Egyptians could not defend themselves from attacks that came from almost every direction.

Statues of Osiris, Isis, and Horus.[10]

Even though there was unrest, everyday Egyptians continued making art. They created statues and paintings. They still worshiped their gods and goddesses, especially Ra, Isis, Osiris, and Horus.

At the end of this period, people no longer believed that the pharaoh was a link between humans and the gods. Instead, Amun was seen as the most powerful god. The priests gained more power. They claimed they were the only ones who could understand Amun's will.

The Third Intermediate Period was the beginning of the end for mighty ancient Egypt. Another power would soon take control.

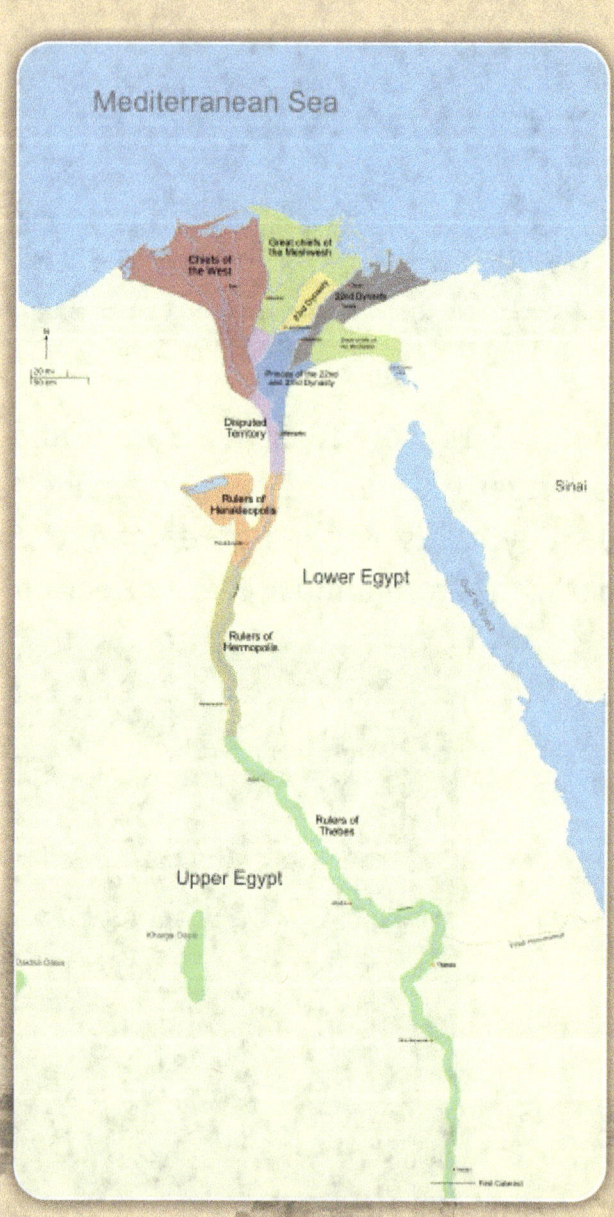

A fractured Egypt during the Third Intermediate Period.[11]

The End of the Egyptian Empire

Although the Egyptians still lived on, their power was never the same again. In 332 BCE, Greek armies led by Alexander the Great won many battles in the region. He built many cities in Egypt. One of the most famous cities was Alexandria, which he named after himself.

The ancient Egyptian empire lasted for nearly three thousand years. It had been ruled by roughly 170 pharaohs. In the end, wars divided the kingdom.

Bust of Alexander the Great.[12]

Alexander the Great conquered Egypt in 332 BCE. He died at the age of thirty-three in 323 BCE.

After Alexander the Great died, his general, Ptolemy (*tah-luh-mee*), and his family ruled Egypt for another three hundred years.

> ## Fun Fact
> " It is believed that Alexander the Great never lost a battle. "

Around 30 BCE, a major change happened in Egypt's history. The Roman Republic took control of Egypt.

Queen Cleopatra VII, the last pharaoh of Egypt, formed an alliance with Mark Antony, a Roman general. Together, they tried to stand against Octavian, another Roman leader who wanted to rule all of Rome.

In 30 BCE, Octavian invaded Egypt. Cleopatra and Mark Antony both died shortly afterward. With their deaths, Egypt was no longer ruled by a pharaoh.

Egypt officially became a province of the Roman Empire. Octavian later became known as Emperor Augustus. He was the first emperor of Rome.

Even though Egypt was now under Roman rule, its culture, religion, and monuments continued to amaze visitors. Roman emperors admired Egypt's wonders and even built temples in the Egyptian style.

> ## Fun Fact
> " Egypt remained an important part of the Roman Empire for hundreds of years. It supplied the empire with grain, gold, and culture! "

Chapter 3 Activity

Are the following statements true or false?

1. The Third Intermediate Period came after the Middle Kingdom.

2. Pharaoh Imhotep was the last king of the New Kingdom.

3. Even during the troubled times of the Third Intermediate Period, the Egyptians still worshiped their gods and goddesses.

4. The Assyrians invaded Egypt from Sudan.

5. Around 331 BCE, the Romans, led by a man named Julius Caesar, won many battles in Egypt.

Chapter 3 Activity Answers

1. False. It came after the New Kingdom.

2. False. Pharaoh Ramesses XI was the last king of the New Kingdom.

3. True.

4. False. The Assyrians came from Mesopotamia.

5. False. Around 331 BCE, the Greeks, led by a man named Alexander the Great, won many battles in Egypt.

Chapter 4: Daily Life in Ancient Egypt

The banks of the Nile River provided the ancient Egyptians with fertile soil that was perfect for growing food. Farming was one of the most important parts of daily life.

Men and women worked together in the fields to plant wheat and barley. They dug canals to bring water from the Nile River to water their fields. At harvest time, everyone pitched in to gather the crops. Farming was hard work, but it helped feed their families and the kingdom.

Ancient Egyptians plowing a field.[13]

Farming was not the only important job in ancient Egypt. They created clothes, cooking utensils, and even jewelry. The Egyptians were skilled in making metal pots and bowls for eating and cooking. They made tools to help them with firing and made weapons for hunting and protection.

Some people made pottery or jars out of clay. Some of this pottery held things like food to protect it from mice. You can still see these ancient jars in museums around the world today!

But life wasn't all work. The Egyptians liked to have fun too. They sang songs, danced at festivals, and played music using harps, flutes, and rattles. Some even sang while working in the fields. Music was a big part of everyday life.

Ancient Egyptians enjoying music and dance.[14]

Children in ancient Egypt loved to play. They played games like tug-of-war and leapfrog. Archaeologists have found toys like dolls, carved wooden animals, and small carts with wheels. Some kids made spinning tops out of stones to play with. These were shaped so that they would spin across the ground.

Families worked hard to make the things they needed. Men and women used a plant called **flax**, which grew along the Nile River, to make thread. That thread was woven into linen fabric for clothes. Most people wore loose, light clothing to stay cool in the hot sun. Rich people wore finer fabrics. Everyone wore sandals made from papyrus and reeds found along the river.

> **FUN FACT**
> "Children usually didn't wear clothes until they were about six years old!"

Ancient Egyptian clothing.[15]

Egyptians also worked together to protect their towns. Soldiers carried weapons like spears, bows and arrows, daggers, and slings. Later on, they built **chariots**. These were fast, two-wheeled carts. Chariots were usually used in battle, but they were also used by royalty to travel in style.

Boats were very important for fishing and travel. Egyptians built small boats out of bundles of reeds and larger warships from cedarwood. Some of their ships had big linen sails. Some of their warships were rowed by up to fifty people!

When people got sick or hurt, they went to a doctor, just like you do today. Egyptian doctors used plants and herbs to make medicine. They also believed in the power of magic. Some doctors called on **Heka** (*heh-kah*), the god of medicine and magic, to help heal injuries and illnesses.

What Did the Ancient Egyptians Eat?

Egyptians grew much of their food along the Nile River. They baked bread using wheat and barley. Their gardens were full of vegetables like garlic, onions, leeks, cucumbers, and melons. They also picked fruits like figs and dates. Ancient Egyptians used grapes to make wine or raisins. Bakers made sweet breads filled with honey and fruit for special treats.

Richer families had more meat, like goose, duck, and goat. Everyone enjoyed fish from the Nile. Poorer families ate more vegetables and bread.

The ancient Egyptians relied on each other to make sure they had enough food and goods.

> **Fun Fact**
> Most Egyptians didn't eat much meat because it spoiled quickly in the heat!

Everyone did their part to make life easier.

Chapter 4 Activity

Fill in the blanks in the following sentences.

1. Flax is a kind of _____ that grew along the Nile River.
2. The ancient Egyptians grew crops like _____.
3. Some Egyptian warships were made of _____.
4. Both men and women wore _____ on their feet.
5. Children in ancient Egypt played games like _____ and _____, just like children do today.

Chapter 4 Activity Answers

1. Plant
2. Wheat and barley
3. Cedarwood
4. Sandals
5. Tug-of-war and leapfrog

Chapter 5: Land of the Pharaohs

To many, ancient Egypt is a land of mystery, mummies, and pyramids. It was all these things and more. For thousands of years, Egypt was ruled by pharaohs. **Pharaohs** were powerful kings and queens who guided their people. They made laws and were in charge of temples and religious festivals.

The Egyptians believed that the pharaoh was the link between humans and the gods. The pharaoh was believed to be all-powerful and wise. The people also believed the pharaoh kept the universe in balance. That balance was known as **ma'at** (*mah-aht*).

Some pharaohs became more famous than others. Let's look at a few.

Djoser (Ruled c. 2670-2648 BCE)

Djoser (*joe-zer*) ruled during the Old Kingdom. He lived in the capital city of Memphis and supported mining and building projects.

Statue of Djoser from the Step Pyramid.[16]

Djoser is best remembered for ordering the construction of the Step Pyramid at Saqqara. This was the first pyramid built from cut stone. Unlike earlier tombs made of mudbrick, his pyramid had four equal sides stacked in six levels. It looked like a giant staircase reaching toward the sky.

Khufu (Ruled c. 2543-2436 BCE)

King **Khufu** (*koo-foo*) also ruled during the Old Kingdom. He is best known for building the Great Pyramid of Giza. The Great Pyramid of Giza is one of the Seven Wonders of the Ancient World. It is the only ancient wonder still standing today!

A small statue of King Khufu.[17]

Historians believe he began ruling in his early twenties and stayed in power during the construction of the pyramid. It took about twenty-three years to complete the pyramid. Though little is known about his life, the giant structure he left behind still amazes visitors today.

Hatshepsut (Ruled c. 1479-1458 BCE)

Hatshepsut was one of the few women who held the title of pharaoh. To make sure people knew she had the strength and wisdom to rule, she was depicted with a fake beard in statues. She ruled for about fifteen years.

Hatshepsut focused on building temples and creating peace through trade. Her ships traveled far across the seas and returned with valuable goods like **ebony** (a precious black wood), gold, and spices. She helped Egypt grow strong without going to war.

Statue of Hatshepsut.[18]

> **FUN FACT**
>
> " One of the most famous temples Hatshepsut helped build is the temple complex at Karnak. She added tall columns, statues, and beautiful carvings to honor the gods. You can still visit what's left of it today and see the amazing work she helped create. "

King Tutankhamun (r. c. 1332-1323 BCE)

Tutankhamun is perhaps the most famous king of Egypt. He is often called King Tut or the Boy King. He was only nine years old when he became king of Egypt. Of course, he had adult advisors to help guide him. He died nine years later at the age of eighteen.

So, why is King Tut one of the most famous pharaohs? In 1922, an archaeologist named Howard Carter discovered King Tut's tomb in the Valley of the Kings. The tomb was filled with treasures, including a golden mask and a set of beautifully decorated coffins. Some of these treasures can still be seen in museums all around the world today.

Carter found the burial chamber of this young king. Inside a **sarcophagus** (*sar-coff-ah-gus*), or stone coffin, were several more coffins, each one slightly smaller and fitting inside the next. The first and second wooden coffins were covered in gold foil. The innermost coffin was made of solid gold. It weighed about 240 pounds!

Funeral mask of King Tutankhamun.[19]

Inside the final coffin was the mummy of the young king. He was buried with beautiful jewelry and magical charms meant to protect him on his journey to the afterlife. Covering his face was a golden mask made in his image. It is one of the most famous treasures ever found.

FUN FACT

> It took Howard Carter nearly ten years of hard work to unearth the treasures of King Tut's tomb.

King Tut didn't have time to do much during his short life, but one important thing he did was bring back the old religion. His father, Akhenaten, had made a big change. He told everyone to stop worshiping all of the gods and instead pray to just one god, Aten, the sun god. This upset many people in Egypt. They believed that praying to only one god would upset the cosmic balance known as ma'at.

There are still rumors about King Tut's death. Some say he was killed. Others believe it was an accident. Most scientists today believe he died from an illness.

Ramesses II (r. c. 1279–1213 BCE)

Ramesses II ruled Egypt for about sixty-six years. That was a very long time for one king to rule! He was also known as Ramesses the Great. He became famous for building massive statues and temples all over the land.

Statue of Ramesses II at Luxor.[20]

Roman bust of Cleopatra VII.[21]

After Caesar's death, Cleopatra became close with one of his top generals, Mark Antony. They became allies and lovers. Cleopatra and Antony joined forces to protect Egypt from the growing power of Caesar's adopted heir, Octavian.

Cleopatra supported Antony in a naval battle against Octavian's fleet. They were defeated at the Battle of **Actium** (*ack-tee-um*) in 31 BCE. The couple escaped to Alexandria. When the Roman forces closed in, Cleopatra and Antony chose to end their lives rather than be captured.

Fun Fact

" Cleopatra wasn't Egyptian by birth. She was of Greek descent. Her family ruled Egypt after Alexander the Great died. Cleopatra loved Egyptian culture. She wore traditional clothing and even learned to speak the Egyptian language. "

> **Fun Fact**
>
> "Ramesses II was made a captain in the Egyptian army at the age of ten! While the title was most likely honorary, he became known for being a brave leader."

He also fought in important battles, especially against the Hittites. After many years of war, he made peace with them and even married a Hittite princess. Ramesses II was admired by his people and is remembered as one of Egypt's greatest pharaohs.

Cleopatra VII (r. c. 51-30 BCE)

Cleopatra VII was the last pharaoh of ancient Egypt. She is also one of the most famous rulers in history. She became the queen after her father died. She took the throne with her younger brother, Ptolemy XIII. The two were married. This was a popular custom among the ruling family at the time.

The two disagreed with each other. Ptolemy tried to take power for himself, and a civil war broke out. He died during the fighting. Cleopatra then ruled with another brother, Ptolemy XIV.

At the same time, the Roman Empire was growing stronger. In 48 BCE, the Roman general Julius Caesar arrived in Egypt after victories in Italy and Spain. He stayed in the city of Alexandria during the winter. Cleopatra met him there, and the two became friends. They later became romantic partners. She even traveled to Rome to visit him. But in 44 BCE, Caesar was killed by some of his own senators.

Chapter 5 Activity

Choose the correct answer in these multiple-choice questions.

1. King Tut is most well-known for what?
    a. His military knowledge and power
    b. Building many temples and pyramids
    c. His tomb, gold coffin, and gold death mask
    d. His ability to lead his people

2. Hatshepsut was one of the few female pharaohs in ancient Egyptian history. She did which of the following?
    a. She ruled for fifteen years.
    b. She encouraged sea trade with her neighbors.
    c. She wore a false beard.
    d. All of the above

3. King Khufu is best known for what?
    a. Building the Step Pyramid
    b. Organizing the first Egyptian army
    c. Building the Great Pyramid
    d. None of the above

4. Ramesses II was famous for doing what?
    a. Being the pharaoh for a long period of time
    b. Building huge statues of himself throughout the land
    c. Marrying the daughter of one of his former enemies
    d. All of the above

Chapter 5 Activity Answers

1. **C.** King Tut is most known for his tomb, his gold coffin, and his gold death mask.

2. **D.** Hatshepsut not only ruled for fifteen years, but she also encouraged trade with her neighbors and wore a false beard!

3. **C.** Little is known of King Khufu except that he built the Great Pyramid of Giza.

4. **D.** Ramesses II was a good and strong pharaoh. He ruled for many years. He married the daughter of the Hittite king. He built large statues of himself that are found throughout Egypt today.

Chapter 6: Egyptology: Mummies and Pyramids

The study of ancient Egypt is called **Egyptology** *(e-gipp-tol-uh-jee)*. People who study ancient Egypt are known as Egyptologists. These experts want to learn everything they can about one of the oldest and most amazing civilizations in history.

When we think of ancient Egypt, we often picture pyramids, mummies, and mysterious tombs. But there's more! Egypt is also famous for its giant temples, towering statues, and colorful wall paintings. Inside many tombs, the walls are covered in **hieroglyphs** *(hi-row-gliffs)*—pictures that stand for sounds and words in the ancient Egyptian language.

Even though no one knows exactly what ancient Egyptian sounded like, scholars believe each picture symbol represents a sound. When put together, they formed words, just like letters do today.

Digging into the Past

Ancient Egyptians were actually the first ones to study their own history. About three thousand years ago, a pharaoh named Thutmose IV told workers to dig out the Great Sphinx, which had been buried in sand. Thousands of years later, people around the world would finally see its full face.

In modern times, Egyptologists have worked hard to uncover the secrets hidden beneath the sands of Egypt. The job hasn't been easy. They have battled heat and sandstorms. Most of the treasure was stolen a long time ago by tomb robbers, which makes it harder to learn more about their culture.

FUN FACT

" Egyptologists are still digging today! Each discovery helps us understand more about the lives, beliefs, and customs of ancient Egypt. "

1860 photograph of the Great Sphinx of Giza.[22]

Famous Egyptologists

Many men and women have spent their lives studying ancient Egypt. One of the most important figures in Egyptology was Sir William Flinders Petrie. He was born in 1853. He is called the "Father of Egyptian Archaeology." Over a hundred years ago, he explored the Egyptian desert and uncovered ancient objects called **artifacts**. Artifacts are ancient tools, statues, and even mummies. Thanks to people like him, we can now see these treasures in museums around the world.

Another famous Egyptologist was Howard Carter. He became famous in 1922 when he discovered the tomb of King Tutankhamun. This pharaoh is also known as King Tut. He was a young pharaoh whose burial site had been hidden for over three thousand years. Inside, Carter found gold, statues, furniture, and a dazzling gold mask made for the boy king.

Egyptologist Howard Carter opens King Tutankhamun's tomb.[23]

Egyptian Curses

When Howard Carter opened King Tut's tomb, some people believed it was protected by an ancient curse. One inscription reportedly warned, "Death will come on swift wings to those who disturb the Pharaoh." After a few team members got sick or died, newspapers called it the "mummy's curse." Scientists today think those events were just bad luck or caused by germs and mold in the tombs.

Still, stories of magical curses and walking mummies capture people's imaginations even today! Stories and movies make people think that mummies can come back to life. But this is just a spooky tale. Ancient Egyptian magic wasn't meant to wake the dead. It was meant to protect them.

What's Inside the Tombs?

It's not just pyramids or tombs that excite people. It's the incredible objects inside them. Archaeologists have found golden masks, carved furniture, tiny statues, and even toys that ancient Egyptians used thousands of years ago.

Egyptologists still work in the Valley of the Kings. The tombs there are decorated with bright paintings. They are filled with treasures that the pharaohs would need in the afterlife. Some tombs have statues of gods, like Anubis. He is the jackal-headed god who protects the dead.

Inside the tomb of Ramesses III.[24]

Mummies

A mummy is a person or animal whose body has been carefully preserved after death. The ancient Egyptians believed that if the body stayed whole, the person could live again in the afterlife. They wanted to make sure the body didn't rot or fall apart, so they used a special process called **mummification** *(mum-if-ih-kay-shun)*.

They believed the soul needed a home to return to, and that home was the body. But preserving a body wasn't easy. It took skill, time, and sacred rituals.

Why Did They Make Mummies?

The Egyptians believed that after death, the soul traveled to the underworld. There, it would face tests before entering the afterlife. One important test involved the heart. The jackal-headed god Anubis would weigh the person's heart against a feather. If the heart was light and free of sin, the person could live forever in peace. If it was heavy with evil, they would be denied the afterlife.

To prepare for this journey, the body had to be well preserved.

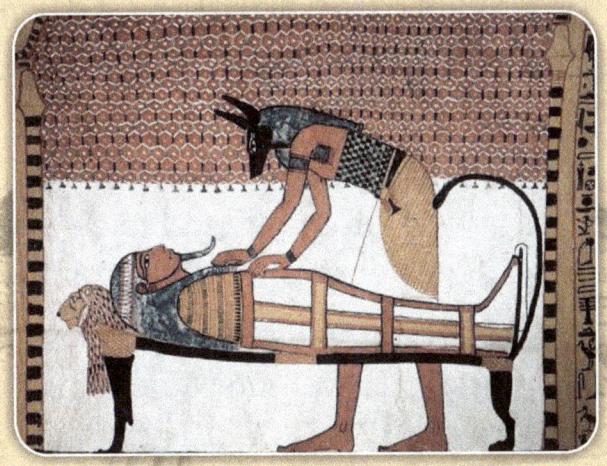

Image of Anubis tending an official of Tutankhamun.[25]

How Were Mummies Made?

Mummification was a careful and sacred process. It took about seventy days to complete. Here's how it worked:

1. Washing the Body: First, the body was cleaned with water, wine, and oils.
2. Removing the Organs: Most internal organs were taken out, except the heart, which Egyptians believed was needed in the afterlife.
3. Removing the Brain: The brain was pulled out through the nose using a hook. Egyptians thought the brain wasn't important.
4. Drying the Body: The body was covered in a special kind of salt called **natron** *(nay-tron)* to dry it out completely. This took about forty days.
5. Stuffing the Body: After the body was dried, the body was filled with linen, leaves, and spices to keep its shape.
6. Oiling and Wrapping: The body was rubbed with oils and then wrapped in long strips of linen cloth.
7. Adding Amulets: Special charms and objects were placed between the linen layers to protect the person in the afterlife.
8. Final Burial: The mummy was placed in a decorated coffin. They were often placed inside more than one coffin. Then, they were buried in a tomb or pyramid.

Thanks to this process, some mummies have lasted over three thousand years! One well-preserved mummy is Seti I, a pharaoh who died in 1279 BCE. His mummy still shows his face clearly thousands of years later!

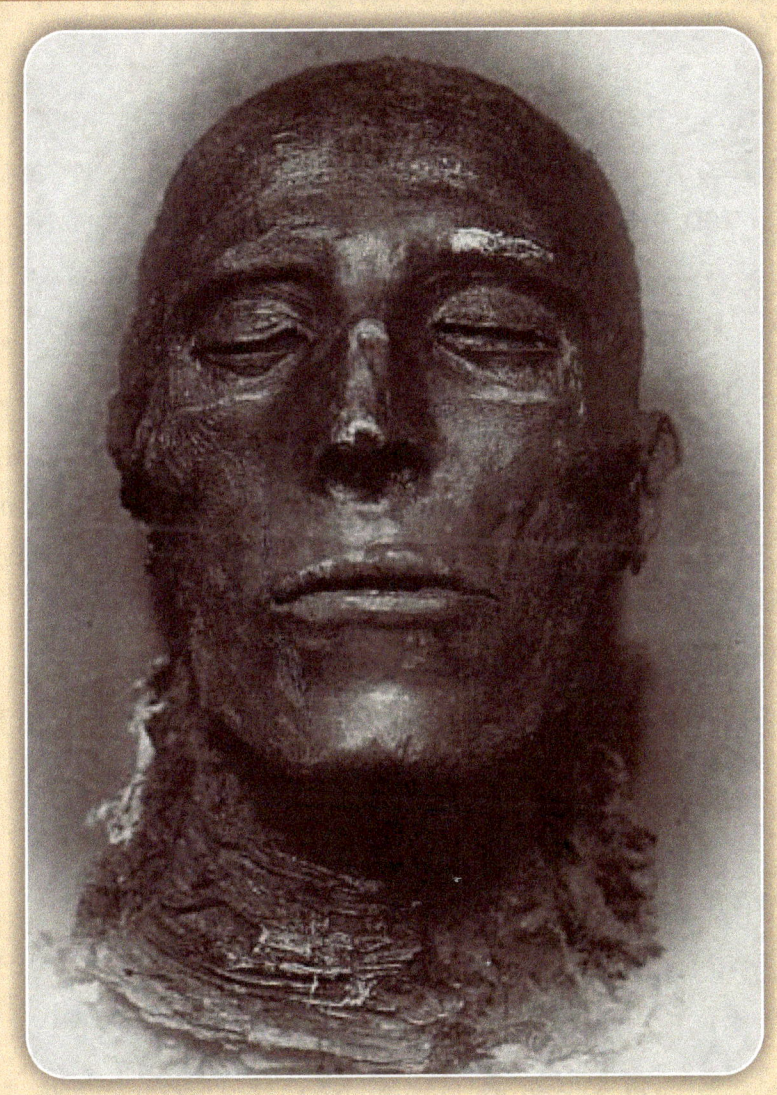

Mummy of Seti I.[26]

Most human mummies were buried in tombs, not pyramids. Pyramids were only used for the richest and most powerful rulers. Pyramids were popular during certain periods, like the Old Kingdom.

> **Fun Fact**
> " Animals were mummified! Cats, crocodiles, and birds went through the mummification process. "

Pyramids

When most people think of ancient Egypt, they picture giant pyramids reaching toward the sky. These amazing stone structures were built thousands of years ago as tombs for pharaohs. But the earliest pyramids looked very different from the smooth-sided ones we know today.

The First Pyramid

One of the first pyramids ever built was the Step Pyramid of King Djoser. It was built around 2630 BCE. It's called a "step" pyramid because it has several levels that rise like stairs. It does not have smooth sides.

This pyramid was the first one made from stone blocks instead of mudbricks. It was a **template** (blueprint) for future pyramids like the ones at Giza.

" Nearly four hundred rooms have been discovered underneath Djoser's Step Pyramid! "

Step Pyramid of Djoser.[27]

How Did They Build the Pyramids?

Building a pyramid was a huge job! It took tens of thousands of workers and about twenty years to build the Great Pyramid of Giza. This was the largest pyramid the ancient Egyptians ever built.

Here's how historians think it might have been done. First, large stone blocks were cut out of nearby quarries. Workers used sleds to drag the blocks across the desert. They might have poured water on the sand to make it firmer and easier to slide the heavy stones.

To lift the stones, workers built a long ramp beside the pyramid. As the pyramid grew taller, the ramp grew. Once the pyramid was finished, the ramp was taken apart.

No one knows exactly how it was done, but these are the best ideas based on tools, artwork, and science.

Fun Fact

" Some estimates say it took around 100,000 workers to build the Great Pyramid! "

The Pyramids of Giza

The Great Pyramid of Giza is the largest of the three pyramids built during the Old Kingdom of Egypt. It was built for Pharaoh Khufu around 2560 BCE. At the time, it stood about 481 feet tall. It was as tall as a 44-story building!

The Great Pyramid of Giza remained the tallest manmade structure in the world for almost four thousand years. It lost this title when the Lincoln Cathedral in England was completed in 1311 CE.

Next to the Great Pyramid of Giza are two other pyramids. One of them was built for Khufu's son, Pharaoh Khafre. The smaller one was built for Pharaoh Menkaure. Khafre's pyramid looks almost as tall as the Great Pyramid because it was built on higher ground. It still has some of its smooth, white limestone casing at the top.

These pyramids are not just ancient tombs. They are wonders of engineering that continue to amaze people today.

Overhead view of the three pyramids of Giza.[28]

Chapter 6 Activity

Find and circle the words in the list below.

C	A	R	T	E	R	S	A	K	P
U	I	M	C	G	M	U	M	M	Y
R	Q	Z	U	L	A	J	T	T	R
S	P	H	I	N	X	S	P	J	A
E	O	T	E	H	E	X	B	E	M
A	X	F	U	O	T	O	M	B	I
W	B	Y	K	S	M	B	W	G	D
H	I	E	R	O	G	L	Y	P	H
L	C	D	T	N	T	I	S	H	R
K	I	N	G	T	U	T	L	E	T

Carter
King Tut
Curse
Pyramid
Mummy
Hieroglyph
Sphinx
Tomb

Chapter 6 Activity Answers

C	A	R	T	E	R				P
U					M	U	M	M	Y
R									R
S	P	H	I	N	X				A
E									M
									I
									D
H	I	E	R	O	G	L	Y	P	H
K	I	N	G	T	U	T			

Chapter 7: Language and Hieroglyphics

The ancient Egyptians used drawings of symbols, objects, and pictures to share information. They were known as *hieroglyphs*. But don't be fooled. If you saw a picture of a bird, it didn't always mean "bird." Each picture could stand for a sound, idea, or even a whole word.

Their full writing system is called hieroglyphics *(hi-row-gliff-iks)*. It is one of the oldest writing systems in the world. Egyptians painted hieroglyphics on walls, carved them into stone, and wrote them on **papyrus**–a kind of paper made from reeds along the Nile River.

Fun Fact

" Hieroglyphs could be written in any direction-left to right, right to left, or even top to bottom! You can tell which way to read it by looking at which way the people or animals are facing. "

Piece of hieroglyphs from the tomb of Seti I.[29]

In the early days, only scribes—highly educated men—could read or write. It took years of training to learn all the symbols. Ancient Egyptian writing included over seven hundred symbols, sometimes even more. By the end of the New Kingdom, more people, including some commoners, could read and write at least a little.

Egyptians wrote with black ink made from soot or charcoal and colored inks made from crushed minerals, like copper for blue and clay for red.

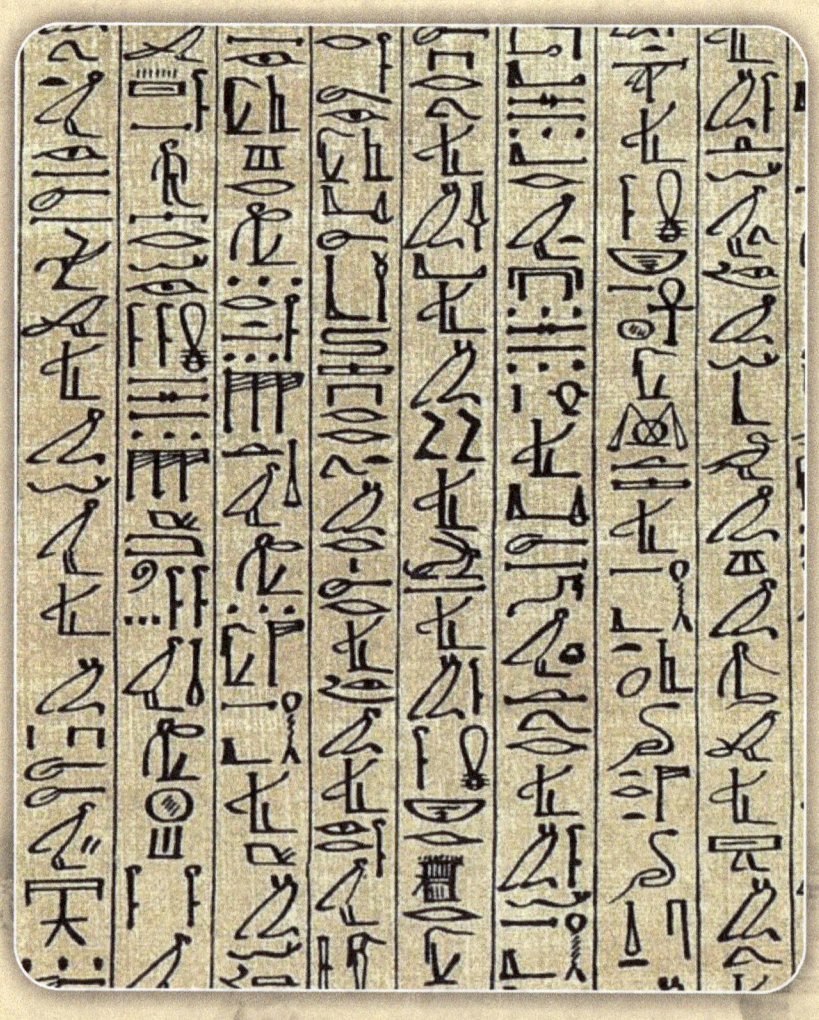

Hieroglyphs on papyrus.[30]

Hieroglyphs weren't just used to decorate tombs. Ancient Egyptians used them to record important events and prayers on the walls of temples and tombs. They also used hieroglyphs to tell stories about their gods, pharaohs, and even their everyday lives.

These symbols could be found on everything from official government documents to beautiful pieces of jewelry and statues. They helped keep track of things like laws, taxes, and supplies.

How Did We Learn to Read Hieroglyphs?

For thousands of years, no one knew how to read ancient Egyptian writing. The meanings of the symbols were lost over time. That changed in 1799 when soldiers near the town of Rosetta discovered something amazing: a stone with writing in three languages! This stone is now called the Rosetta Stone.

Rosetta Stone.[31]

The Rosetta Stone is a big piece of black granite. It is about four feet tall and two feet wide. It has the same message written in three scripts:

- Hieroglyphics
- Demotic (a simpler, everyday Egyptian script)
- Ancient Greek

The message is about a ceremony for Ptolemy V, a Greek ruler of Egypt. He ruled from around 204 BCE to 180 BCE. Because scholars could read Greek, they could use the Rosetta Stone as a guide to figure out what the hieroglyphs meant. After more than twenty years of studying it, they finally began to crack the code of this ancient language.

Chapter 7 Activity

Circle the right answer.

1. The Rosetta Stone is a _____.
   a. Piece of jewelry worn by Cleopatra
   b. A small chunk of rock
   c. A description of a ceremony printed on papyrus
   d. A stone with different languages on it

2. Roughly how many different objects or signs were used by the ancient Egyptians in their writing?
   a. 250
   b. 575
   c. 700
   d. 1,000

3. Each object or picture had a different _____.
   a. Meaning
   b. Tone
   c. Rhythm
   d. None of the above

4. In order to finally figure out what the Rosetta Stone said, the scholars first translated what language?
   a. German
   b. French
   c. Greek
   d. Macedonian

Chapter 7 Activity Answers

1. **D.** A stone with different languages on it.

2. **C.** About seven hundred original symbols or signs were used in the ancient Egyptian language.

3. **A.** Every symbol or object in Egyptian hieroglyphics had a different meaning.

4. **C.** The ability to translate the Greek language on the Rosetta Stone allowed researchers to finally understand hieroglyphs.

Chapter 8: Mythology: Gods and Goddesses

Ancient Egypt is sometimes called the Land of the Gods—and for good reason! The Egyptians believed their world was guided by powerful gods and goddesses who controlled everything around them. They believed these gods made the sun rise, the crops grow, and the rivers flood. The gods were a part of daily life, from birth to death and beyond.

> **Fun Fact**
> "The ancient Egyptians worshiped over two thousand gods! They had a god for just about everything, including good luck and knowledge."

These gods and goddesses were part of Egyptian **mythology**—a collection of stories passed down for generations to explain how the world worked and what happened after death.

Ra – The Sun God

Ra *(rah)* was the sun god. He was one of the most important gods in ancient Egypt. He was shown with the head of a falcon and a glowing sun disk on top. The Egyptians believed that Ra sailed across the sky during the day in a golden boat. At sunset, his boat sank beneath the earth, and he traveled through the underworld at night. The next morning, Ra rose again—just like the sun!

Ra, the Egyptian sun god.[32]

Anubis – The God of the Dead

Anubis, the god of the dead.[33]

Anubis *(uh-new-bis)* had the head of a **jackal**, a wild dog often seen near tombs. He was the protector of the dead. He helped guide souls safely to the afterlife. Anubis also oversaw the mummification process. Egyptians believed he watched over their loved ones even after death.

> ### Fun Fact
> Because jackals were seen in cemeteries, the Egyptians believed they had a special connection to the afterlife.

Isis – The Protector

Isis.[34]

Isis *(eye-sis)* was one of the most beloved goddesses in ancient Egypt. She was known for her powerful magic and healing skills. She was the wife of Osiris and a protector of children, mothers, and the dead. People looked to her for comfort, guidance, and protection.

Thoth – The God of Wisdom

Thoth.[35]

Thoth *(toth, like "both")* was the god of knowledge, writing, and the moon. He looked like a man with the head of an **ibis**, a long-beaked bird. He was the smartest of all the gods and often helped settle arguments between them. Thoth was also in charge of judging souls. He helped weigh the hearts of the dead to decide their fate.

Osiris – Ruler of the Underworld

Osiris.[36]

Osiris *(oh-sigh-ris)* ruled the underworld. He was known as the Lord of the Dead. Osiris had green skin, which symbolized life and rebirth. After death, Egyptians believed their heart would be weighed by Thoth and judged by Osiris. If they had lived a good life, they could move on to the afterlife.

But if their heart was heavy with evil, they faced a terrible fate. They would be eaten by Ammit *(am-ee-it)*, a fearsome creature with the head of a crocodile, the front of a lion, and the back of a hippopotamus!

Image of Ammit.[37]

Fun Fact

" Egyptians believed a pure heart was lighter than a feather—literally! "

The Egyptians looked to their gods for answers about life, death, and nature. From the rising sun to the flooding of the Nile, the gods were always watching and helping guide their world.

Chapter 8 Activity

Find the words in the word search based on the clues listed below. (If you can't figure out the answer, review the chapter once more. The answers are listed on the next page.)

1. Anubis was the god of the dead and had the head of a _____.

2. Osiris was known as the Lord of the _____.

3. This god of the moon was said to have the head of an _____.

4. The sun god of ancient Egypt was named _____.

5. This goddess was the wife of Osiris.

m	r	l	q	i	r	j
y	t	n	z	b	a	a
t	i	e	l	j	k	c
h	d	e	a	d	i	k
w	p	d	k	r	s	a
a	m	l	h	t	i	l
z	i	b	i	s	s	x

65

Chapter 8 Activity Answers

1. Jackal
2. Dead
3. Ibis
4. Ra
5. Isis

						r	j
						a	a
							c
	d	e	a	d		i	k
						s	a
						i	l
	i	b	i	s	s	s	

Chapter 9: Forty Fun Facts About Ancient Egypt

In this chapter, we will share some fun and interesting facts about ancient Egypt. Some of these facts are funny, weird, or just very interesting.

1. Each side of a pyramid faces one of the four **cardinal points** found on a compass. The cardinal points are north, south, east, and west. Each side was the exact same length. The corners formed perfect right angles.

2. The Red Pyramid is about 344 feet tall. The Pyramid of Khafre stands around 448 feet tall. The Great Pyramid of Giza is now 455 feet tall, though it was originally even taller. It used to be 481 feet tall!

3. Anubis was believed to be the god that offered protection to the dead. He is often shown with black paint, which symbolized rebirth in the afterlife. Even though he was connected to death, he was not seen as evil.

A statue of Anubis from the tomb of King Tutankhamun.[38]

4. The name of a dead person was written inside their tomb so they would be remembered forever.

5. Several major ancient Egyptian cities were built along the banks of the Nile River. The modern city of Luxor stands where the ancient city of Thebes once thrived. It was the capital during the New Kingdom and is still home to amazing temples and tombs that tourists can visit today!

6. Hatshepsut was one of ancient Egypt's earliest and most powerful female pharaohs. To show her authority, she was often portrayed as a **sphinx**—a creature with a lion's body and a human head. She also wore a false beard, just like the male pharaohs did.

7. King Tutankhamun, more commonly known as King Tut, died when he was eighteen or nineteen years old. Scientists believe he might have died from a mix of malaria, a bone disease, and a serious leg injury.

8. The ancient Egyptians invented the first toothpaste. It was made out of slightly burned eggshells, ashes, or even ox hooves that were ground into powder. Yuck! They made their breath smell good with a mixture of honey and cinnamon.

9. Napoleon Bonaparte encouraged archaeological expeditions in Egypt in 1798. His team found the Rosetta Stone!

10. About 330 pharaohs ruled Egypt over roughly 3,000 years.

11. After someone was mummified, their organs were placed in special jars called canopic jars. Each jar was protected by a different god. One jar had a jackal head and guarded the stomach. Another had a baboon head and protected the lungs. A third, with a falcon head, watched over the intestines. The fourth jar had a human head and protected the liver.

12. Ancient Egyptians made their houses out of mudbricks baked by the sun. A good worker could probably make one thousand bricks a day!

13. Pharaohs often wore a crown with the head of a cobra on the front of it. The cobra was believed to protect the pharaoh from harm.

14. Each stone block of the Great Pyramid of Giza weighed as much as a hippopotamus (an average of three thousand pounds)!

15. Many wealthy or powerful Egyptians shaved their heads and wore wigs, which were sometimes held on with beeswax. They believed this kept them clean and cool in the hot Egyptian sun.

16. Ancient Egyptians believed in a heaven-like place known as the Field of Reeds. Only people who had been good in life could go there after death.

17. It could take several days to wrap a single mummy!

18. The famous Bent Pyramid wasn't actually bent. It was called that because its slopes had two different angles. This likely happened due to instability during the building process.

The Bent Pyramid.[39]

19. Hundreds of yards of linen strips were needed to wrap one mummy.
20. Pyramids were not generally built by slaves. Scholars believe paid laborers built them.
21. Egyptians timed planting and harvesting around the yearly flooding of the Nile River.

Painting inside the tomb of Nakht.[40]

22. The ancient Egyptians believed that evil spirits caused illnesses. Magic spells and garlic were typical treatments.

23. About three hundred thousand cat mummies were found in the Temple of Bastet! Bastet was a goddess with the head of a cat.

24. Ancient Egyptians believed their dreams were messages from the gods.

25. Ancient Egyptians invented one of the earliest types of locks and keys. They used them to protect doors and storage boxes.

26. Modern technology discovered that Ramesses III had been murdered.

27. Women in ancient Egypt had more rights than in many other ancient cultures. They could own property, manage businesses, and go to court.

28. The ancient Egyptians were pet lovers. They kept many household pets, including cats, dogs, and monkeys!

The Temple of Karnak.[41]

29. Men and women in early Egypt wore makeup. They believed it gave them the protection of gods, such as Ra and Horus.

30. The ancient temple in Karnak is one of the largest temple complexes in the world.

31. Burial chambers inside tombs were filled with things a person might need in the afterlife. Food, clothing, and even games were placed in the tombs.

32. The crook and the flail were the two most common symbols of a pharaoh's power and authority.

Crook and flail.[42]

33. The pharaohs' long braided beards were mostly fake. Some were even made of metal! They were often tied on with a ribbon or a chin strap. The beards were designed to imply their status as a living god.

34. About 118 pyramids were built by pharaohs. The pyramids served as their tombs.//
35. The Nile River is one of the longest rivers in the world. It is about 4,132 miles long!
36. Most of Egypt is covered by the Sahara Desert. The desert covers about 3.3 million square miles.
37. The Valley of the Kings is the site of over sixty-five royal tombs. Many pharaohs of the New Kingdom were buried there.
38. Children in ancient Egypt didn't go to school like we do today, but they still found time for fun. They played with toys like dolls, spinning tops, balls, and board games. One popular game was Senet, a game of strategy and luck that adults played too.
39. The mummy of King Tutankhamun was discovered wearing more than one hundred pieces of jewelry, including a false finger and toe protectors made of gold.
40. Because bad breath was common due to tooth decay, the ancient Egyptians created the first "breath mints." They were made of honey, cinnamon, myrrh, and frankincense. They were shaped into pills.

Which fact were you most shocked at? Which fact will you share at dinner tonight with your family?

Chapter 9 Activity

Go back through this book to see if you can find five to ten more interesting things you learned about ancient Egypt!

1. _____
2. _____
3. _____
4. _____
5. _____
6. _____
7. _____
8. _____
9. _____
10. _____

Conclusion

The land of ancient Egypt has fascinated people of all ages for hundreds of years. It is a place of vast deserts and the mighty Nile River. It is a land of powerful pharaohs, towering pyramids, and mysterious mummies.

For more than three thousand years, the ancient Egyptians ruled parts of northern Africa. Each period of their history brought new ideas and achievements. They created beautiful art and amazing buildings. Their rich religious beliefs shaped their lives.

Today, millions of people visit Egypt's ancient temples and pyramids each year. Museums around the world display statues, jewelry, and mummies that were once part of this incredible civilization. We read books, watch movies, and explore websites filled with the wonders of ancient Egypt.

We hope you've enjoyed exploring this incredible land from long ago. But this is just the beginning. There are still so many mysteries and stories waiting to be discovered. So keep learning, keep exploring, and keep traveling through the ancient past!

If you want to learn more about tons of other exciting historical periods, check out our other books!

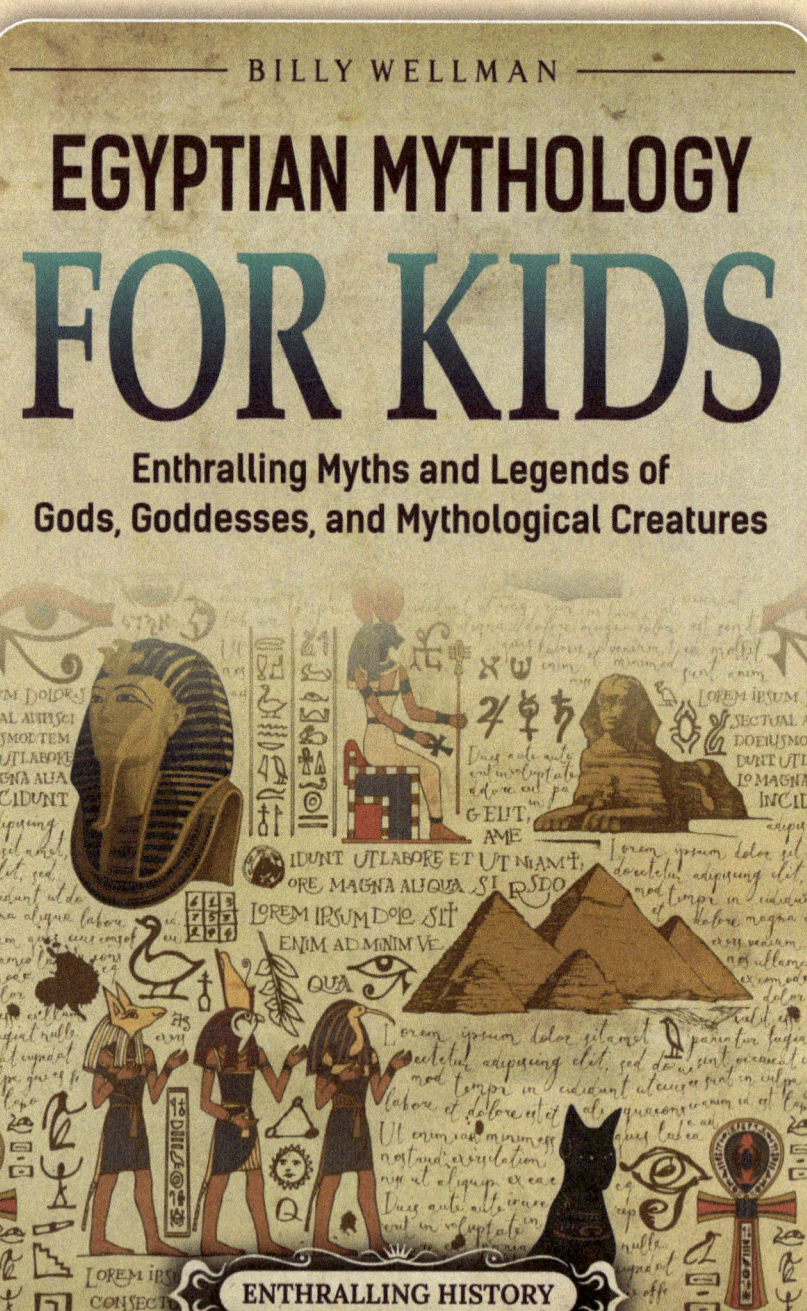

Books to Check Out

We hope this is just the start of your adventures into the past. Here are some books we think you might find interesting:

Boyer, Crispin. *National Geographic Kids Everything Ancient Egypt: Dig Into a Treasure Trove of Facts, Photos, and Fun.* 2012.

Captivating History. *Ancient Egypt for Kids: A Captivating Guide to Egyptian History from the Early Dynastic Period through the Early, Middle, and Late Kingdom to the Death of Cleopatra.* 2021.

Cook, Hugo. *Tales of Ancient Egypt: Myths & Adventures from the Land of the Pyramids.* 2024.

DK. *Ancient Egypt.* 2025.

References

Journey to the Past – Ancient Egypt. Solbiati, Romano. 2001, Steck-Vaughn Publishers, New York.

Ancient Egypt – A Look at Ancient Civilizations. Faust, Daniel R. 2019, Gareth Stevens Publishing, New York.

Daily Life in Ancient Egypt. Nardo, Don. 2002, KidHaven Press, San Diego, CA

Ancient Egypt – Technology in Times Past. Snedden, Robert, 2009, Smart Apple Media/Black Rabbit Books, Minnesota.

Ancient Egypt: Scholastic Discoveries. Arlon, Penelope. 2014, Scholastic Inc., New York.

Ancient Egypt: The Great Discoveries. Reeves, Nicholas. 2000, Thames & Hudson, New York.\

Archaeology Hotspot Egypt: Unearthing the Past for Armchair Archaeologists. Heath, Julian. 2015. Rowman & Littlefield, New York.

Nile River: https://education.nationalgeographic.org/resource/nile-river/.

Sumerians. https://www.khanacademy.org/humanities/world-history/world-history-beginnings/ancient-mesopotamia/a/mesopotamia-article.

Elam: https://www.worldhistory.org/article/1591/ten-ancient-elam-facts-you-need-to-know/.

Mentuhotep II. https://www.britannica.com/biography/Mentuhotep-II.

King Tut: https://www.smithsonianmag.com/history/how-howard-carter-discovered-king-tuts-golden-tomb-180981052/.

The Rosetta Stone: https://www.britannica.com/topic/Rosetta-Stone.

Image Sources

[1] BabelStone, CC BY-SA 3.0 <https://creativecommons.org/licenses/by-sa/3.0/>, via Wikimedia Commons; https://commons.wikimedia.org/wiki/File:Early_writing_tablet_recording_the_allocation_of_beer.jpg

[2] Kasid12, CC BY-SA 4.0 <https://creativecommons.org/licenses/by-sa/4.0>, via Wikimedia Commons; https://commons.wikimedia.org/wiki/File:Ancient_Egyptian_old_and_middle_kingdom.png

[3] Olaf Tausch, CC BY 3.0 <https://creativecommons.org/licenses/by/3.0>, via Wikimedia Commons; https://commons.wikimedia.org/wiki/File:Sakkara_12.jpg

[4] Daniel Mayer, CC BY-SA 4.0 <https://creativecommons.org/licenses/by-sa/4.0>, via Wikimedia Commons; https://commons.wikimedia.org/wiki/File:Giza_Plateau_-_Great_Sphinx_-_front_view.JPG

[5] Juan R. Lazaro, CC BY 2.0 <https://creativecommons.org/licenses/by/2.0>, via Wikimedia Commons; https://commons.wikimedia.org/wiki/File:Mentuhotep_II_Deir_el_Bahri.jpg

[6] I, Sailko, CC BY-SA 3.0 <https://creativecommons.org/licenses/by-sa/3.0>, via Wikimedia Commons; https://commons.wikimedia.org/wiki/File:Amenemhet_III,_basalto,_seconda_met%C3%A0_del_XIX_sec._ac._01.JPG

[7] Andrei Nacu, Jeff Dahl, CC BY-SA 3.0 <https://creativecommons.org/licenses/by-sa/3.0>, via Wikimedia Commons; https://commons.wikimedia.org/wiki/File:Egypt_NK_edit.svg

[8] https://commons.wikimedia.org/wiki/File:Abu_Simbel_Temple_May_30_2007.jpg

[9] Osama Shukir Muhammed Amin FRCP(Glasg), CC BY-SA 4.0 <https://creativecommons.org/licenses/by-sa/4.0>, via Wikimedia Commons; https://commons.wikimedia.org/wiki/File:Ashurbanipal_II%27s_army_attacking_Memphis,_Egypt,_645-

635_BCE,_from_Nineveh,_Iraq._British_Museum.jpg

[10] Louvre Museum, CC BY-SA 2.0 FR <https://creativecommons.org/licenses/by-sa/2.0/fr/deed.en>, via Wikimedia Commons; https://commons.wikimedia.org/wiki/File:Jewel_Osiris_family-E_6204-IMG_0641-gradient.jpg

[11] Jeff Dahl, CC BY-SA 4.0 <https://creativecommons.org/licenses/by-sa/4.0>, via Wikimedia Commons, https://commons.wikimedia.org/wiki/File:Third_Intermediate_Period_map.svg

[12] https://commons.wikimedia.org/wiki/File:Alexander_the_Great_Ny_Carlsberg_Glyptotek_IN574_n1.jpg

[13] https://commons.wikimedia.org/wiki/File:Maler_der_Grabkammer_des_Sennudem_001.jpg

[14] https://commons.wikimedia.org/wiki/File:Musicians_and_dancers_on_fresco_at_Tomb_of_Nebamun.jpg

[15] https://commons.wikimedia.org/wiki/File:Ancient_Times,_Egyptian._-_001_-_Costumes_of_All_Nations_(1882).JPG

[16] Prof. Mortel, CC BY 2.0 <https://creativecommons.org/licenses/by/2.0>, via Wikimedia Commons; https://commons.wikimedia.org/wiki/File:Detail_of_statue_of_Djoser_from_Step_Pyramid_Complex_at_Saqqara,_2630-2611_BCE;_Egyptian_Museum,_Cairo_(2).jpg

[17] Olaf Tausch, CC BY 3.0 <https://creativecommons.org/licenses/by/3.0>, via Wikimedia Commons; https://commons.wikimedia.org/wiki/File:Kairo_Museum_Statuette_Cheops_03_(cropped).jpg

[18] Keith Schengili-Roberts, CC BY-SA 2.5 <https://creativecommons.org/licenses/by-sa/2.5>, via Wikimedia Commons; https://commons.wikimedia.org/wiki/File:Hatshepsut-CollosalGraniteSphinx02_MetropolitanMuseum.png

[19] Roland Unger, CC BY-SA 3.0 <https://creativecommons.org/licenses/by-sa/3.0>, via Wikimedia Commons;

https://commons.wikimedia.org/wiki/File:CairoEgMuseumTaaMaskMostlyPhotographed.jpg

[20] Merlin UK, CC BY-SA 3.0 <https://creativecommons.org/licenses/by-sa/3.0>, via Wikimedia Commons; https://commons.wikimedia.org/wiki/File:Luxor_Temple_-_panoramio_(10).jpg

[21] https://commons.wikimedia.org/wiki/File:Kleopatra-VII.-Altes-Museum-Berlin1.jpg

[22] Rijksmuseum, CC0, via Wikimedia Commons; https://commons.wikimedia.org/wiki/File:The_Sphinx_and_great_pyramid._Geezeh,_RP-F-F25403-K.jpg

[23] https://commons.wikimedia.org/wiki/File:Tuts_Tomb_Opened.JPG

[24] R Prazeres, CC BY-SA 4.0 <https://creativecommons.org/licenses/by-sa/4.0>, via Wikimedia Commons; https://commons.wikimedia.org/wiki/File:KV11_Tomb_of_Ramses_III_DSCF2941.jpg

[25] https://commons.wikimedia.org/wiki/File:Anubis_attending_the_mummy_of_Sennedjem.jpg

[26] https://commons.wikimedia.org/wiki/File:Pharaoh_Seti_I_-_His_mummy_-_by_Emil_Brugsch_(1842-1930).jpg

[27] https://commons.wikimedia.org/wiki/File:Saqqara_stepped_pyramid.jpg

[28] Robster1983 at English Wikipedia, CC0, via Wikimedia Commons; https://commons.wikimedia.org/wiki/File:Giza-pyramids.JPG

[29] https://commons.wikimedia.org/wiki/File:Hieroglyphs_from_the_tomb_of_Seti_I.jpg

[30] https://commons.wikimedia.org/wiki/File:Papyrus_Ani_curs_hiero.jpg

[31] British Museum, CC BY-SA 4.0 <https://creativecommons.org/licenses/by-sa/4.0>, via Wikimedia Commons; https://commons.wikimedia.org/wiki/File:Piedra_Rosseta.JPG

[32] Jeff Dahl, CC BY-SA 4.0 <https://creativecommons.org/licenses/by-sa/4.0>, via Wikimedia Commons; https://commons.wikimedia.org/wiki/File:Re-Horakhty.svg

[33] Jeff Dahl, CC BY-SA 4.0 <https://creativecommons.org/licenses/by-sa/4.0/>, via Wikimedia Commons; https://commons.wikimedia.org/wiki/File:Anubis_standing.svg

[34] Jeff Dahl, CC BY-SA 4.0 <https://creativecommons.org/licenses/by-sa/4.0/>, via Wikimedia Commons; https://commons.wikimedia.org/wiki/File:Isis.svg

[35] Jeff Dahl, CC BY-SA 4.0 <https://creativecommons.org/licenses/by-sa/4.0/>, via Wikimedia Commons; https://commons.wikimedia.org/wiki/File:Thoth.svg

[36] Jeff Dahl, CC BY-SA 4.0 <https://creativecommons.org/licenses/by-sa/4.0/>, via Wikimedia Commons; https://commons.wikimedia.org/wiki/File:Standing_Osiris_edit1.svg

[37] Jeff Dahl, CC BY-SA 4.0 <https://creativecommons.org/licenses/by-sa/4.0/>, via Wikimedia Commons; https://commons.wikimedia.org/wiki/File:Ammit.svg

[38] https://commons.wikimedia.org/wiki/File:Tutankhamun_jackal.jpg

[39] CC BY-SA 4.0 <https://creativecommons.org/licenses/by-sa/4.0/>, via Wikimedia Commons; https://commons.wikimedia.org/wiki/File:Bent_Piramidi.jpg

[40] https://commons.wikimedia.org/wiki/File:Tomb_of_Nakht_(2).jpg

[41] Gerd Eichmann, CC BY-SA 4.0 <https://creativecommons.org/licenses/by-sa/4.0/>, via Wikimedia Commons; https://commons.wikimedia.org/wiki/File:Karnak-02-Uebersicht_mit_heiligem_See-1982-gje.jpg

[42] Jeff Dahl, CC BY-SA 4.0 <https://creativecommons.org/licenses/by-sa/4.0/>, via Wikimedia Commons; https://commons.wikimedia.org/wiki/File:Crook_and_flail.svg